EXPLORING HISTORY

The Edwardians

SYDNEY WOOD

Oliver & Boyd

Contents

Topics for Workguides

Oliver & Boyd
Robert Stevenson House
1–3 Baxter's Place
Leith Walk
Edinburgh EH1 3BB

A Division of Longman Group Ltd

First published 1981

ISBN 0 05 003349 2

Printed in Hong Kong by
Sing Cheong Printing Co Ltd

Introduction

The people in the picture opposite are members of the Atkinson family. The photograph was taken in the year 1906 when Britain's King was Edward VII. Edward became King when his mother, Queen Victoria, died in 1901. Though he himself died in 1910 the whole period up to 1914 is often called *Edwardian Times*.

1. *What clues are there in the picture that tell you it was taken many years ago?*
2. *Do you think these people were quite well off? Give a reason for your answer.*

In the picture on the right, too, you can see some children. Like those in the first picture, they lived in Edwardian times.

1. *Why do you think some of these boys are not wearing shoes and socks?*
2. *What sort of shop do you think they are looking at?*

In Edwardian times there were quite a number of people who were very well off: there were also many who were very poor. In this book you will be able to find out much more about how all sorts of different people lived by looking at what they wrote and at photographs that were taken then.

In Edwardian times people used 'old' money.
12d. (pennies) equalled 1s. (shilling)
20s. (shillings) equalled £1.
£1 then would buy very much more than it does now, as you will see as you read this book.

1. A Fashionable Life

The King

Edward had to wait until he was fifty-nine years old before he became King. This is what Wilfred Blunt, a poet, wrote about him.

He had a passion for dressing up, and he was never tired of putting on uniforms and receiving princes and ambassadors and opening museums and hospitals and attending cattle shows and military shows and shows of every kind, while every night of his life he was to be seen at theatres and operas and music halls.

(Quoted in Nowell-Smith *Edwardian England*)

The King loved good food and wine and entertaining company. He was fond of sports, especially horse racing – indeed in 1909 his own horse, Minoru, won the Derby. In Victoria's later years, court life had seemed serious, even gloomy. Many people admired the lively change brought about by Edward. His wife, the Danish princess Alexandra, quietly put up with her husband having affairs with a series of beautiful ladies like Mrs Keppel and Lily Langtry.

1. *What do the pictures (left and opposite) show that Edward VII was interested in?*
2. *What other things does Wilfred Blunt mention as the King's interests?*
3. *Do you think you would have admired Edward if you had been living then? Say why.*

King Edward's life-long love of sport helped his popularity. Here he poses with his Derby winner, Minoru.

The Rich

Beatrice Webb remembered that when she was a rich young Edwardian lady she spent her time

Riding, dancing, flirting and dressing-up – in short entertaining and being entertained . . . the presentation at Court, the riding in the Row [*a fashionable place in London*], the calls, the lunches and dinners, the dances and Ascot.

My Apprenticeship

1. *List the various ways in which a rich young lady of fashion spent her time.*
2. *Describe what you think Beatrice Webb meant by the calls.*

The King's rich friends were often landowners with titles, though some were people who had made their money from trade and business. One Edwardian said:

Thirty or forty years ago millionaires were somewhat of a rarity and were spoken of with a certain amount of wonder. Now they are counted by the score.
(Quoted in D. Read *Edwardian England*)

A great deal of cheap foreign food was imported. This cut down the profits of British farmers. Landowners were often glad, therefore, to accept and intermarry with the 'new' rich. Edward himself was especially friendly with Sir Thomas Lipton who had made a fortune from his grocery businesses.

1. *Explain in your own words who the two groups were who made up the rich class of society. Where did their wealth come from?*

Passing the Time

Edward VII was easily bored. Like other fashionable people, he seemed to be constantly on the move. From May to July London was the centre of entertainment for the rich. But there were country houses he visited, too (they were often huge, with over 100 rooms). Wealthy society-people stayed at Cowes for the yachting, visited Henley for the rowing, Ascot for horse-racing, and went abroad, especially to Southern France and Monte Carlo.

While it was an honour to entertain Edward, his hosts had to keep him constantly amused. The wealthy Marchioness of Curzon remembered

We always had a large house party for Ascot Races and all our friends had people staying with them too, and there were dinner parties and balls every night. These full days of gaiety

King Edward (right) deer stalking in the Scottish Highlands. Rich people often owned large houses in this part of Britain, visiting them for the shooting and fishing seasons.

involved frequent rapid changes of dress. The Life Guards used to give a ball in their barracks and there were many other excellent dances. Of course we often went to parties in London. At Windsor we rode and danced and also played lawn tennis and golf.

Memoirs

1. *List all the different ways of spending time that were outdoor activities.*
2. *Find and list all the different indoor entertainments mentioned here.*
3. *How many servants do you think a house like the one below would need?*
4. *What sorts of different jobs would they have to do?*

Chatsworth House in Derbyshire is a fine example of the sort of enormous country house visited by Edward VII and by other wealthy guests of the owners. A vast private park surrounded the house.

Food

You can see from the photograph at the beginning of this chapter that the King was quite a big man. He was very fond of food, but so too were many fashionable Edwardians. Sir Harold Nicolson remembered what breakfast was like in a house such as Chatsworth.

They ate excessively. Rows of little spirit lamps warmed rows of large silver dishes. On a table to the right were grouped Hams, Tongues, Galantines (cold white meat, boiled and spiced), Cold Grouse, Pheasant, Partridge, Ptarmigan. There would also be a delicate rectangle of pressed beef. On a further table stood fruits and jugs of cold water and of lemonade. A fourth table contained porridge utensils. A fifth, coffee and pots of Indian and China tea. The centre table would be bright with toast racks.

Small Talk

The day contained not only a large lunch and an elaborate evening dinner, but afternoon tea as well.

1. *Write down a list of things you usually have for breakfast. Next to it write down a list of the things to be seen at an Edwardian breakfast for the wealthy.*
2. *How many large meals in a day did rich Edwardians eat? How many do you have?*
3. *Who do you think prepared, served, cleared away and washed up to make these meals possible?*

Servants

Edward VII and his fashionable friends could live as they did because there were so many servants to attend to their needs. In 1910 two million women earned their livings as servants. Many thousands of men were in domestic service too. Here is the kind of life that was lived by one servant, Alice Cairns.

I had to clean the big range and get the fire going before I could boil a kettle. And then I used to scrub the big kitchen which had a floor like gravestones and scrub the tables and then take the cook a cup of tea before 7.0 am. Then I had to clean the servants' hall. They were very rich people. They used to have huge dinners which used to go on till 10 or 10.30 before dinner was over and me, being the in-between maid, had all the washing-up to do and all the vegetables to clean. We had one day a month off.

(Quoted in *The Long March of Everyman*)

Alice would only earn about £12 a year. It would be many years before she could expect to get £30 as a head housemaid, and she would never equal the earnings of a butler, who might receive £100 a year.

1. *How many hours work in a day did Alice Cairns probably do?*
2. *Why do you think she put up with such a hard life?*

You will find a note about money on page 3.

In their work of cleaning, making fires, preparing and cooking food, washing up, washing and ironing clothes, there were few modern gadgets to make life easier for servants. It was hard work keeping all the coal fires, solid fuel stoves and oil lamps going. Newer houses had electric light, and gas lighting was common in well-to-do homes. More and more gadgets were beginning to appear, however, in Edwardian times.

1. *Why could the machine in the advertisement only be afforded by the rich?*
2. *Servant's rooms were at the top and bottom of great houses. Why do you think this was?*
3. *Do you think the bed in the second picture would be comfortable?*
4. *The rich employed servants to care for their children. Why do you think this was?*
5. *Do you agree with this sort of treatment of children? Does it still happen today in Britain?*

Led by their King, fashionable Edwardians had a very rich and varied life. It did not matter to them that this life depended on the labour of thousands of servants.

B·V·C
PORTABLE CLEANER

I CLEAN THE WHOLE HOUSE IN ONE DAY

Get Rid of the Dust
by using the British Portable Vacuum Cleaner, which thoroughly removes all dust from Carpets, Drapery, Upholstery, and Furniture, without discomfort to the household.

Prices { HAND MACHINES, £6 6s.
{ ELECTRIC ,,   from 16 to 50 Gns. }

THE BRITISH VACUUM CLEANER CO., Ltd.,
96, Parson's Green Lane, London, S.W.

(top) Portable electric vacuum cleaners cost around £35 by 1906. The wealthy employed servants to do their cleaning – as the advertisement shows. Ordinary people could not afford such machines.

(bottom) Folding beds were very suitable for the small attic rooms in which servants commonly lived.

2. A Comfortable Life

Inside Fir Tree House

Homes

In this picture we can see inside part of the home of the Atkinson family. (A picture of this family is on page 2.) Fir Tree House was probably a very comfortable and pleasant home. The Atkinsons even had a central heating system put in which lasted for seventy years!

The Atkinsons were members of the middle class. This group included people earning as little as £150 a year up to people with incomes of at least £2000.* They worked at all sorts of jobs. Shopkeepers, clerks, teachers, businessmen, lawyers and doctors were all middle class.

A pleasant home and garden was a sign that a family had reached the middle class. A London clerk, Robert Thorne, thought that the home he was struggling to pay for showed he was not working class.

In front was a privet hedge and a tiny flower bed under the parlour bay window: at the back was a small garden. You will see that we were finding our feet in the social world making the best show we could. The brass knocker, the bay window, the dining and drawing room, established the fact, whilst the study gives evidence that already we had in view the great suburban ideal of being superior to the people next door. I know it gave Nell great satisfaction to discuss the vices and virtues of her servant (she was of the kind called 'Daily' and cost us half-a-crown a week) with the neighbouring

* You will find a note about money on page 3.

ladies, and to dispense afternoon teas in the drawing room.

(Quoted in D. Read *Documents*)

1. What parts of his home was Robert Thorne especially proud of?
2. Why do you think Mrs Thorne liked to talk about her servant?

Servants

Like all other middle class people, the Atkinsons had servants in their home. Life was becoming more comfortable. They had electric as well as gas lighting, bathrooms – usually with waterclosets – and more machines to make cleaning and washing easier. But servants were still thought to be essential. In 1901 the *Cornhill Magazine* advised couples setting up home on an income of £800 a year.

Having taken your house and put down £130 of your £800 for rent, the next question is the number of servants. Two is the right number, a cook at £20 a year and a house-parlourmaid at £18. If a woman marries on £800 a year she ought not to be too proud to lend a constant head and occasional hand to the conduct of the house. Her husband should be his own butler, the wife should dust the china and ornaments.

1. What do you think the writer means by lend a constant head?

2. What actual work in the home were this couple going to do? Does it seem to be a heavy burden of work?

The Suburbs

Mr Atkinson was a builder with a business in Leeds. In 1904 he moved his family out to Huby, fourteen kilometres from Leeds, and settled down to live in Fir Tree House. He could still get to Leeds easily, for there was a railway station near his new home. All over Britain other middle-class families were moving away from city and town centres too. In a Birmingham newspaper, for instance, a writer recorded that the middle-class

Like the Arabs are folding their tents and stealing silently away in the direction of Knowle and Solihull.

Birmingham Mail, 1903

By Edwardian times travel had become much easier (see chapter 6). Middle-class people moved away from noisy and smoky areas to places that were more peaceful and where they could own a garden. Whole areas of middle-class housing, called *Suburbs*, grew up.

1. Why did suburbs grow in Edwardian times?

Shopping

Mrs Atkinson must have often caught the train to Leeds too. She would go shopping.

ANDREW COLLIE & COY

The shop and delivery cart of Andrew Collie, a grocer in Cults on the outskirts of Aberdeen. The well-to-do had their grocery orders delivered to their homes.

The writer Arnold Bennett said shopping was very popular with the middle-class.

When they have nothing to do they say in effect, 'Let's go out and spend something.' And they go out. They spend their lives in spending. They deliberately gaze into shop windows in order to discover an outlet for their money.

(Quoted in D. Read *Documents*)

There were plenty of small local shops serving customers individually and delivering purchases to middle-class homes.

1. *Why was shopping so important to the middle-class?*
2. *Do you think men or women cared most about shopping? (Give a reason for your answer.)*

City and town centre shops grew in size and number. The *Fortnightly Review* noticed the growth of a new sort of shop that contained

the gathering under one roof of all kinds of goods – clothing, millinery, groceries, furniture, in fact all the necessities of life.

In 1909 Gordon Selfridge opened a store in London that tried to make shopping even more attractive and comfortable. He said

In my store women can realise some of their dreams, they come here as guests, not customers to be bullied into buying.

(Quoted in *Life in Edwardian England*)

1. *How was shopping starting to change by Edwardian times?*
2. *How do you think Gordon Selfridge probably fitted out and decorated the inside of his store?*

The staff who served in the shops often worked eighty hours in a week. Only in 1912 did they get the right to half-day holidays and then, because the shop-day was so long, they often did not begin until 4.0 pm.

The middle-class Edwardians lived very comfortable lives. They read newspapers, supported libraries, theatres and concerts. Many of Britain's churches and chapels depended on middle-class people to lead them. The taxes they had to pay were few and small in size. Servants were easily obtained and did not need to be paid much.

3. A Hard Life

Homes

In Edwardian times Robert Roberts was a boy living in a shop in a Salford slum like the Liverpool one in the photograph. This is how he described his home area.

The homes of the very poor contained little or no furniture. They made do with boxes and slept in their clothes. In among the respectable rows of 'two up and two down' houses, we had blocks of hovels sharing a single tap, earth closet and open midden: each house with a candle for light, an oil lamp or a bare gas-jet. Coal the 'low class' rarely bought: they picked or stole it.

Roberts remembered a very special day in 1910.

On my mother's insistence, the landlord installed a cast-iron bath (one shilling a week on the rent). Several customers asked to be allowed to inspect it. My father took them on a conducted tour, pointing out the hot and cold taps and the purpose of plug, chain and overflow pipe.

The Classic Slum

1. *What sort of furniture did very poor homes contain?*
2. *How were such homes lit?*

3. *Why do you think the neighbours were so eager to see the Roberts' bath?*

One water pump served the working class inhabitants of this Liverpool Street.

Dr Alfred Salter described housing in part of London

It was a cold day but the family was so poor that they had not even a penny to put into the gas meter for heat. The house was one up and one down with a small scullery and no backyard except for a shut-in paved area three feet [*almost a metre*] deep. Drying and washing was done in the front court where there was one standpipe for twenty-five houses with the water on for two hours daily. There was no place to wash in. There was one water closet for the twenty-five houses.

(Quoted in A. F. Brockway *Bermondsey Story*)

1. *How many rooms did the house have that Dr Salter visited?*
2. *What do you think the front court was?*
3. *How easy was it for the family living there to get water?*

Inside the Home

In his part of Salford Robert Roberts saw

Oilcloth was much in demand, even if one could only afford enough to cover a kitchen floor as far as the furniture. Most families had a rag hearth rug. From some shops you could buy the basic 'House of Furniture' designed to fill the one up and one down home. Most people kept what they possessed clean. Women wore their lives away washing clothes in heavy iron-hooped tubs, scrubbing wood and stone.

The Classic Slum

1. *How were Salford slum floors covered?*
2. *How was clothes-washing done?*
3. *What sort of objects do you have in your home that these people did not have?*

In 1913 Mrs Pember Reeves visited such a home and wrote afterwards

The single room inhabited by this family is large – fifteen feet by thirteen [*about $4\frac{1}{2} \times 4$ metres*]. Under the windows facing the door is the large bed in which sleep mother, father, and two children. At the foot of the bed is a small square table. Three wooden chairs and a chest of drawers complete the furniture. The small fireplace has no oven. There is no larder. On the floor lies a piece of loose linoleum.

(Quoted in P. Keating *Into Unknown England*)

1. *How would having no larder affect the lives of the family?*
2. *What sort of cooking was possible in such a room?*

This London family's sad expressions show their plight: they have run out of money and food.

The wandering poor

Some people had no homes at all. William Booth, the founder of the Salvation Army, heard from his officers reports of the many people who wandered London's streets. One was this man, who was found on the Embankment and said,

I've slept here two nights. I'm a confectioner by trade. I got turned off because I'm getting elderly. They can get younger men cheaper. I thought I could get a job at Woolwich so I walked there but could get nothing. I found a bit of bread in the road wrapped up in a bit of newspaper. That did me for yesterday. I'm fifty-four years old. When it's wet we stand all night under the arches.

(Quoted in P. Keating
Into Unknown England)

1. *Why did the tramp lose his job?*
2. *Why did the tramp not catch the tram to Woolwich?*
3. *What did he do at night when it rained?*

Clothes

The clothes worn by the Salford poor were carefully described by Robert Roberts.

All clothes were made to last, many designed to later meet the needs of successive younger members of the family. Men's outerwear was never really cleaned; some who worked in offensive trades, smelled abominably and

Two of Britain's thousands of wandering poor – asleep in St James's Park, London. Finding a dry safe place to sleep was not easy.

people would avoid the public houses where they gathered. Tradesmen took pride in wearing stiff collars. Women and children wore clogs. A man or woman walking the streets hatless struck one as wretchedly poor. When they could, the very poor wore more clothes – two old shirts, three waistcoats, or even a second pair of trousers. In this way they kept warm and had extra pockets for anything picked up.

The Classic Slum

1. *Why were clothes made to last as long as possible?*
2. *Why did men working in smelly jobs not change to go out in the evening?*
3. *Why did poor people wear several layers of clothes if possible?*
4. *Describe in your own words the sort of clothes women wore.*

Food

Roberts could see from the way people came to the family shop that local people could only buy small amounts of food at a time. They could not afford to travel to distant shops but went to the local one. Not all shopkeepers were careful. Some sold food more like this one,

His sugar is grey and gritty and does not sweeten well; his margarine is strong, he rarely seems to stock the well-known brands, but some species he shapes with butter pats behind a screen. His bacon is always rancid, his cheese second-rate, his cocoa is mixed with cornflour, his jam consists of the refuse from the good jams.

The Classic Slum

1. *What were the dangers in buying food from this shop?*

This is what a family in the area where Roberts lived had for its meals,

Breakfast – Bread and butter, a little cheese, strong tea. *Dinner* – Bread, strong tea, butter or jam. *Supper* – A slice or two of bread and tea.

Some families managed bacon quite often, some could not even afford butter. Poor people in the country could at least grow a few vegetables for themselves.

1. *List the different foods this family ate.*
2. *What is missing from this list that you would expect to eat regularly yourself?*

Mary Pickford, one of the stars of the 'silent' cinema screens of Edwardian times.

Away from it all

The hard life lived by poor people did not have very many bright moments in it. Robert Roberts described one of the most popular escapes from working life.

To the great mass of manual workers the local public house spelled paradise. After the squalor from which so many men came there dwelt within a tavern all one could crave for – warmth, bright lights, music, song, companionship. Above all men went for the ale that brought a slow fuddled joy. Beer was indeed the shortest way out of the city.

The Classic Slum

1. *Why was the public house so attractive?*
2. *What do you think the last sentence means?*

From 1896 cinema shows of silent films grew rapidly from being travelling entertainments in hired buildings, to having special buildings of their own. A pianist played music to suit the action on the screen.

In Robert Roberts' Salford

The cinema burst like a vision into the underman's existence. The world suddenly expanded. Often captions broke into the picture with explanations. When picture gave place to print a muddled chorus of children's voices rose from the benches, piping above the piano music.

The Classic Slum

1. *What sort of sound accompanied silent films?*
2. *What do you think Roberts meant by saying the world suddenly expanded?*

Helping the Poor

Near to Robert Roberts' home stood a large building

behind high walls, housing all those who had abandoned hope in this world. This building could house 2000 people and similar ones could be found all over Britain. These were the workhouses, the last refuge of people unable to stay alive any other way. They were paid for from a poor-rate paid by better-off people in groups of parishes called *Unions*.

The Classic Slum

The Poplar Workhouse in London was visited by George Lansbury. This is what he wrote.

It was easy for me to understand why the poor dreaded and hated these places, all these prison-sort of surroundings were organized for the purpose of making decent people endure any suffering rather than enter. Sick and aged, lunatics and babies and children, able-bodied and tramps, all herded together in one huge range of buildings. Clothing was of the usual workhouse type, plenty of corduroy and blue cloth. No undergarments for either men or women, boots were worn till they fell off. On one visit I inspected the supper of oatmeal porridge served up with pieces of black stuff floating around. We discovered it to be rat and mice manure.

(Quoted in *The Workhouse*)

Some poor people stayed at home or with relatives and were helped by the authorities. A group of officials reported in 1905 on what they found these people were being given.

The lowest scale that we have come across grants each adult only 1s. a week and five pounds of flour. More usual is to find the scale allowing 2s. 6d. per week for an adult. For each child one Union still gives only 6d. and five pounds [*about 2½ kg*] of flour, others 1s. and a loaf.

Royal Commission on Poor Laws

These women eating their dinner in St Pancras Workhouse are dressed in workhouse clothes and strictly organised.

The people who asked for help were checked very carefully by an inspector to make sure they had no money.

1. *What were the buildings called that very poor people were sent to live in?*
2. *Why do you think the people in the picture on page 15 are all dressed alike?*
3. *What sort of people could, according to Lansbury, be found in these places?*
4. *What was the usual amount paid to the poor in their homes as* outdoor *relief?*

Wages

People living in poverty were not just a tiny part of Britain's population. Seebohm Rowntree, the son of a wealthy York chocolate manufacturer, studied both his own home town and reports on London's poor gathered by Charles Booth (a Liverpool shipowner). He decided that almost a third of the population were very poor.

The wages paid for unskilled labour in York are insufficient to provide food, shelter, and clothing adequate to maintain a family of moderate size in a state of physical efficiency.

He worked out that 21s. 8d. a week would just keep a family of five out of real poverty, though the family

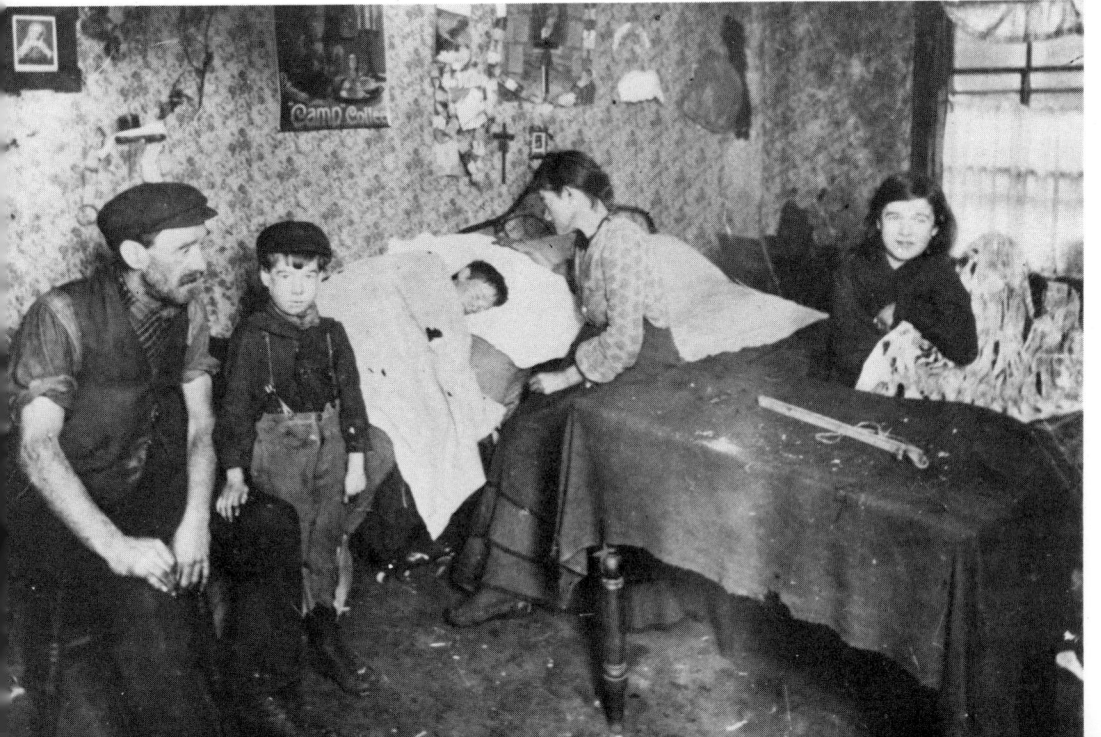

Sad attempts have been made to decorate this room where a family lives with one of the children unwell. Most people had to pay for a doctor's attention and were very reluctant to call for help.

must never spend a penny on railway fare or omnibus. They must never go into the country unless they walk. They must never purchase a newspaper or a ticket for a popular concert. They must write no letters. They cannot save. The children must have no pocket money. The father must smoke no tobacco and must drink no beer. The mother must never buy any pretty clothes. The wage earner must never be absent from his work for a single day.

A Study of Town Life

1. *What did Rowntree decide was an important cause of poverty in York?*
2. *List the various things the family just avoiding poverty had to do without. How does their life compare with yours?*

4. At School

Robert Roberts enjoyed going to his local school, even though there were many things wrong with it.

Year after year inspectors condemned our great sooty building, the unqualified staff, the stinking rooms. But I found it delightful. Some of us went on learning eagerly, a few of the staff showing themselves kindly, human, even gifted teachers.

He overheard school inspectors grumbling that

We had been drilled into a sort of slavish passivity, the teacher addressed us and we did nothing but listen. Free speech didn't come easily to children kept down at home and in the classroom.

A Ragged Schooling

1. *What was wrong with the school building Roberts went to?*
2. *What was wrong with some of the teachers?*
3. *What do you think* slavish passivity *means?*

Elementary Schools

The school in the photograph, like the one Robert Roberts went to, was an elementary school. Most children went to schools like this, leaving as soon as possible to start work. There were few secondary schools, and they charged most of their pupils fees and so were mainly for the better-off.

Some children could leave quite early if they did well enough in their tests. Winifred Spence remembered:

I left school at twelve. I left in the morning and I started work in the afternoon. I was glad when I passed my labour certificate to be out earning some money.

(Quoted in *The Days That We Have Seen*)

1. *What was the earliest age at which children could leave school?*
2. *What do you think the Labour Certificate was supposed to show?*

These pupils at Flint School, London in 1908 sit at sturdy desks fitted with slots for ink-pots and pens.

Headteachers of elementary schools had to write down the main things that happened in their school, every week, in *School Log Books*. These are some of the things written by the Head of Elgin West End School in 1903.

September 25th. Attendance has been very good, weather has improved. Boys of St III had a nature knowledge walk while the girls were attending cookery.

October 28th. Some of the pupils have been sent bramble gathering by their mothers.

November 23rd. Boots purchased by General Anderson's fund given out today.

November 29th. Bar-bell drill has been taken for the Senior Girls, Indian Clubs exercise for the boys.

December 16th. About 50 free tickets were distributed among needful children for the Soup Kitchen.

(Moray District Archives, Forres)

1. *How can you tell that some children at this school were poor?*
2. *Pupils were sent to gather brambles [blackberries] in schooltime. What other sorts of rural activities would upset attendance at school?*
3. *Attendance improved when the weather did. Why do you think the weather affected going to school far more than it does today?*
4. *Look back to the picture of Flint School. How was classroom furniture different from today's?*

The 1902 Education Act

In 1902 the Conservative Prime Minister, Arthur Balfour, grumbled

The educational system of this country is chaotic, is utterly behind the age, makes us the laughing stock of every advanced nation.

(Quoted in D. Read *Documents*)

Mr Balfour took steps to see that schools were run out of the rates, and to build more schools. This came about under the 1902 Education Act.

Secondary Schools

In 1905 there were 94 000 pupils in state-aided secondary schools.

Very poor children sometimes only went to school for half a day. They were known as half-timers. These children are leaving the mill where they work for the rest of the day.

In 1914 there were 200 000 pupils in state-aided secondary schools.

In 1909 three-quarters of all 14–17 year olds received no form of education.

1. *What do these figures show was happening to secondary schools in Edwardian times?*

In secondary schools then, pupils were taught:

English Language and Literature, at least one Language other than English, Geography, History, Mathematics, Science and Drawing, manual work and physical exercise.

Public Schools

Wealthy people sent their sons to public schools. The boys usually lived in the school, which would charge the parents high fees.

The writer Rudyard Kipling described one of them,

Ten years at an English public school do not encourage dreaming. George won his growth under a system of cricket, football and paper chases.

(Quoted in *Life in Edwardian England*)

At his fee-paying school Llewelyn Woodward remembered,

I had no idea why I was learning Greek or Latin. It rarely occurred to me that once upon a time Greek and Latin were spoken languages. From the first to the last hour of my school-

days I was not given any instruction in the physical or biological sciences.

(Quoted in *Life in Edwardian England*)

Not all public schools were like this, though. A few were encouraging mathematics, science, modern languages, history and geography.

Worry about Britain's position in the world had helped bring about the 1902 Education Act. But in 1914 Britain still lagged a long way behind the USA and Germany in providing technical and scientific education, and University and college education of any sort.

1. *Did most pupils in Edwardian times go to secondary schools?*
2. *What sort of activities were many public schools keen on?*

Few Edwardian pupils experienced a science lesson like this one taking place at Fulham County Secondary School in 1910.

19

5. At Work

Before 1914 apprenticeships of any kind were not generally open to the children of the labouring poor. One had to be 'spoke for', and usually tradesmen spoke only for the sons of tradesmen.

Part-timers in shops lucky enough to be taken on fully after leaving school often enough put in a seventy-four hour week to bring home five or six shillings* to grateful parents.

Many skilled workers used boys, not as apprentices, to assist them. There were those in boot factories who placed the tacks ready for the soling machines. There were lads in the glassworks on twelve-hour shifts taking bottles to the blowers. We had youngsters who spent their teenage years almost wholly engaged in fetching beer for thirsty bricklayers.

In more modern factories, mass-producers had quickly seen the advantages to be gained from the use of juvenile labour. One sewing machine factory managed to turn out its ware with only four or five skilled adult workers to every hundred adolescents, all of whom were sacked before they reached twenty. There were jobs in foundry, ironworks, and shipyard, many of which led youth nowhere except to dismissal on approaching manhood and a place among the mass of unskilled labourers fighting for jobs of any sort.

Robert Roberts *The Classic Slum*

1. Explain what apprenticeships are.
2. Who usually got them?
3. How long did boys in shops usually work?
4. What sort of jobs did boys do to help skilled men?
5. Why do you think factories often sacked boys when they reached twenty years of age?
6. If parents were grateful for an extra 5s. to 6s. a week, what does this tell you about their lives?

* You will find a note about money on page 3.

A factory shop floor in the early 1900s: too many British factories were operating out-of-date machines.

Look at the table on the right.

1. Counting men and women together, what kind of work employed the most people?
2. Is this work still as important today?
3. Did most Edwardians work in farming or manufacturing industry and mining?
4. What was the most important industrial work?

Small Workshops

Edwardian Britain still contained many small workshops. A visitor to a Birmingham craft workshop run by Joseph Brown saw men making all sorts of special metal tools and wrote

He manufactures a great number of different patterns and declared his readiness to execute any of which a design was supplied. All the men are skilled. Everybody works very quickly here. Work begins at 7.0 every day except Sunday and leaves off at 7.0 at night except Saturday when it ends at 2.0 pm. Work is interrupted for two hours for meals. However each workman does not make up this number of hours every week. One never arrives before 9.0 am. Wages are high. I noticed weeks at £2 8s. while nearly all came to £2.

P. de Rousiers *The Labour Question in Britain*

1. How many hours would a man working a full week at Brown's put in?
2. Do you think factory workers would be allowed to come in two hours late? Why was this easier to accept in a small workshop?

Small craft workshops were finding it difficult to make things as cheaply as factories. In Edwardian times, for instance, factory production of footwear increased rapidly, putting out of work many small footwear businesses.

(Now would be a good time to do question 1 in Workguide 5A.)

Women at Work

Women also worked in small workshops making metal objects (such as nails and chains). At such a place

One of the workwomen said that she could usually earn 5s. a week. Another stated that working from seven in the morning till seven at night she could make a hundredweight [*about 50 kg*] of chain in a week for which she was paid from 4s. to 6s. 6d.

(Quoted in *Human Documents of the Age of the Forsytes*)

Coal Mining

In 1906 Thomas Jordan, aged fourteen, started work in the pit. Afterwards he remembered:

The coal seam was about five feet [*about 152 cm*] high. There were railroads leading into places where men hewed and filled. My dad was adamant that I go to the pit. I will earn

	Number of people employed
Agriculture	988 340
Building	945 875
Coal Mining	648 944
Cotton manufacture	582 119
Woollen manufacture	236 106
Iron and steel	216 022
Domestic service for women	1 691 000
Domestic service for men	141 000
Tailoring	259 292
Boot and shoemaking	251 143
Distributive trades (i.e. shops, cafes, pubs)	930 000

The table shows some of the more important kinds of work done by ordinary people at the beginning of Edwardian times.

6s. 6d. a week there. Dressed up as a little miner in a blue flannel shirt, short breeches and strong shoes, on a cold winter night I descended the mine. It was 9.0 pm. and I might ascend the shaft at 8 am. I was a 'trapper boy', pulling open and shutting a door to allow the putters to come through with their ponies and coal tubs. I must stay in this position until relieved.

(Quoted in Burnet *Useful Toil*)

1. How was the coal cut from the seam?

2. How was coal moved from the seam?
3. What work did Thomas Jordan do?

Coal provided heating for homes, fuel for the country's industry (and some of its transport) and one tenth of the value of all British exports. In Edwardian times mining expanded. By 1911 there were 877 000 miners, the most the industry was ever to employ – indeed from 1881 to 1911 the number of miners doubled.

Textiles

Textiles, especially cotton, provided half of all the country's exports.
When Ellen Gill started work at the local cotton spinning mill she had to be there by 6.0 am and stay till 5.30 pm, with one and a half hours for meal breaks. She remembered

My wages were 2s. 6d. per week while I was learning, which turned out to be until somebody either left or died. I was there over a year before there was a vacancy when I was given a place at the bottom of the mule [*machine for spinning cotton*] at 7s. a week.

(Quoted in Burnet *Useful Toil*)

1. Is the mill in the picture for spinning or weaving?
2. Does it seem to need many people to work the machines?
3. Why do you think Ellen Gill accepted such poor pay?

An Airdrie cotton mill, 1907. Textiles employed thousands of women amid a deafening clatter of machinery.

Farming

Edwardian farming used many horses. In Aberdeenshire (at Huntly) a farmer's son, Norman Halkett, recalled,

I was a child when I learned how to groom a horse, how to harness it and how to walk up and down the long rigs alongside your favourite ploughmen listening to his songs and watching. The love which these horsemen had for their animals was quite extraordinary.

   (Quoted in *The Days That We Have Seen*)

1. What sort of farming work do these two pieces of evidence (the extract and the top picture) tell you was done by horses?
2. What does this sort of work today?

Harvest time (top) Horse-power still dominated the countryside in the 1900s.
(bottom) Steam-threshing in Suffolk.
The arrival of the travelling machine was a great occasion on the farm.

This is how James Thrower started working life.

I became a feeder, feeding the corn into the thrashing drum. I got a fork stuck through my hand more than once. We had to walk to work. I walked 108 miles [*about 174 km*] one week.

   (Quoted in *The Days That We Have Seen*)

1. What work are the people in the bottom picture doing?
2. What is steam power being used for? Did this work need many people too?
4. What dangers were there in this work?
5. How is this work done today?

(To find out something about Edwardians at play do Workguide 5B.)

6. Travelling About

These maps only show part of the rail network, but what they tell you applies throughout Britain.

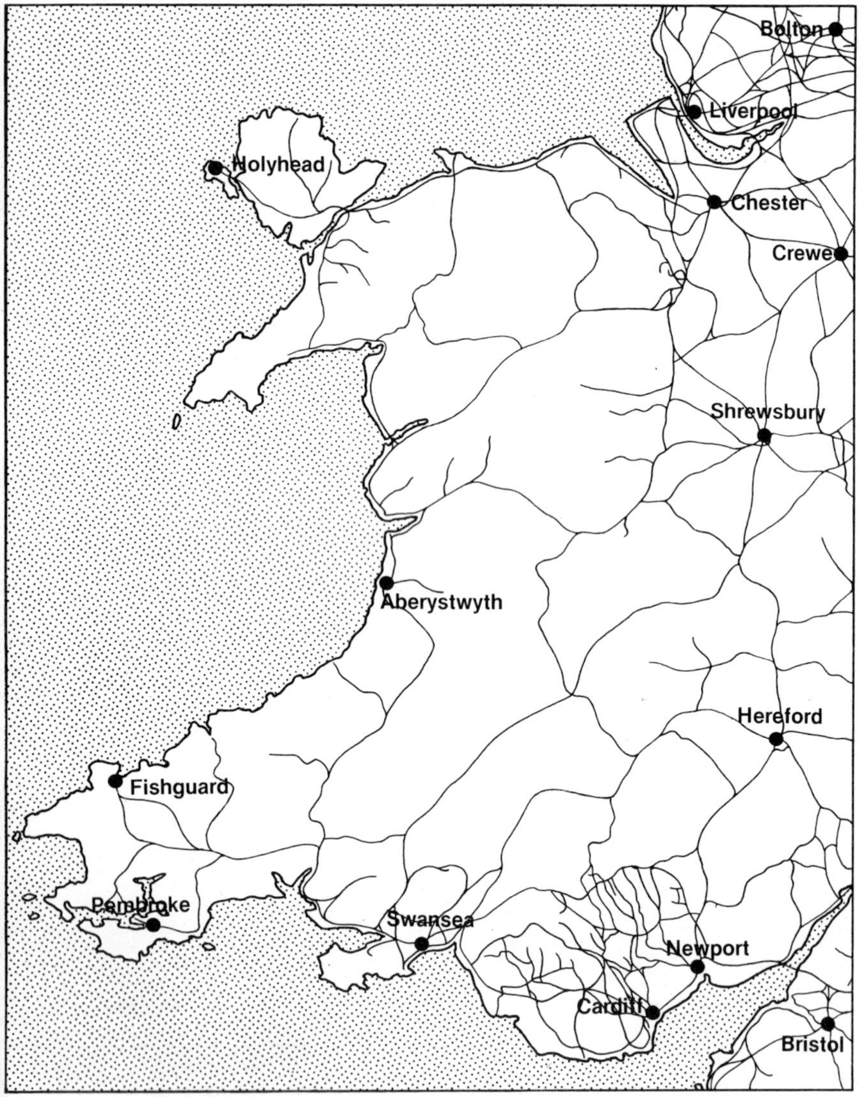

A railway network of Edwardian times (Wales – more important lines only)

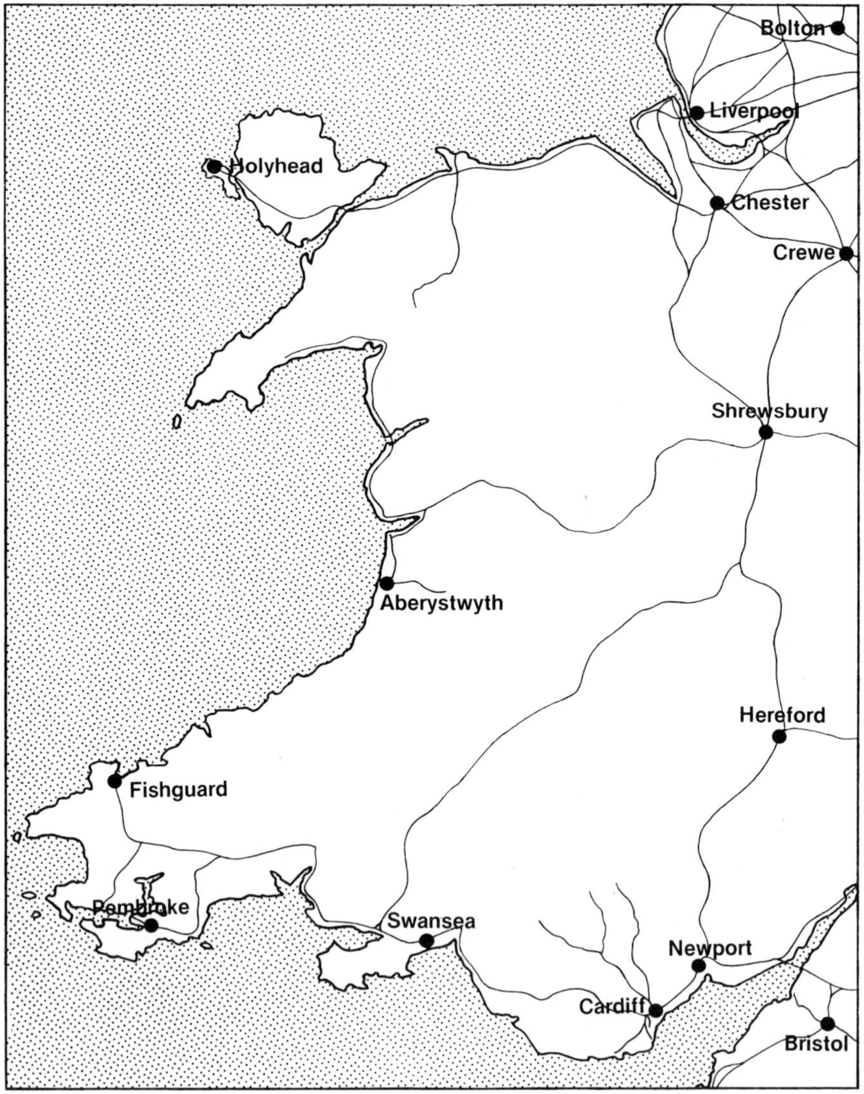

The same area's *complete* railway network today.

1. *Look at the maps. How is the Edwardian railway system different from today's?*

The Underground

By 1901 London's Underground Railway system had grown considerably since the first line opened in 1863. A railwayman of the time remembered

In the tunnels steams and sulphur were the order of the day. The locomotives were small and powerful. They had no cab, only a weatherboard [*a board over the place where the driver stood*]. The traffic was very heavy in the rush hour. The Central London Railway opened in 1900 as the 'Twopenny Tube'. The early trains were hauled by electric locomotives.

(Quoted in *ILN Social History*)

1. *Why were tunnels full of steam and sulphur?*
2. *Would steam and sulphur be a nuisance on the Central London Railway?*

After a number of years, London's tube trains were gradually electrified. The system had an escalator working at its Earls Court Station, from 1911. People were so afraid of it at first, that a man with a wooden leg was paid to ride up and down the escalator to prove its safety!

Horse power

By Edwardian times railways extended everywhere. But this did not ruin the horse-drawn traffic business. In 1901 there were three and a half million horses in Britain.

1. *What sort of jobs could horse-drawn vehicles do that railways could not manage?*
2. *Would railways have hurt the traffic on long-distance main roads, and at the inns on the main roads? Give reasons.*

Cycling

Cycling clubs flourished. Gentlemen were advised to wear the proper cycling clothing. *The Etiquette of Good Society* recommended:

Bicycles were briefly popular with the fashionable – as here, near Hyde Park, London – but motor cars soon reduced them to a means of travel for the less well-off.

Knickerbockers and a short coat buttoned up the front, stockings ribbed and knitted of thick wool, shoes with stout soles, a cap with peaks at the front and back. A light silk handkerchief loosely tied around the neck should take the place of a stiff collar.

(Quoted in *Human Documents of the Age of the Forsytes*)

By 1890 John Dunlop had developed a pneumatic tyre to replace solid tyres. Gears and free-wheeling devices were added. A reasonable cycle could be bought for £5.

1. Do you think ordinary working people could afford bicycles? Why do you think this was?

Horse-drawn vehicles and electric trams mingle on Blackfriars Bridge, London.

Trams

1. What sort of power drives these trams?
2. Are they free to go anywhere their driver chooses? Why is this?

Robert Roberts believed

The introduction of all-electric trams in cities during the first years of the century greatly influenced the lives of the common people. As early as 1903 horse-drawn trams vanished from the streets of Manchester. Electric trams would now take passengers three-quarters of a mile for a half penny and more than two miles [*3 km*] for a penny. In summer loads of children were to be seen rattling along the rails en route for fields and parks, and innumerable families experienced the pleasure of day trips; journeys were half as dear and twice as fast as those made on the old horse trams. The electric tramcar enabled more working-class people than ever before to find a job beyond their immediate neighbourhood, to visit relatives and friends, to go to parks, libraries, theatres, concerts, cinemas, museums, schools and technical colleges.

The Classic Slum

1. What sort of trams were used before electric ones?
2. Why were electric trams an improvement?
3. List three different ways in which trams altered people's lives.
4. Do you think any horse-drawn traffic would have suffered from the arrival of electric trams? Give a reason for your answer.

Motor vehicles

Time was when you could escape from the pressure of work and pass some quiet delightful hours. Now all is altered. The motor cars fizz and roar by the dozen. They monopolise every road and street. All this develops the spirit of unrest and hurry.

Letter in *The Illustrated London News*, 1903

1. What was the effect of cars on people's lives?

Cars were made by many small companies in Britain such as Napier and Lanchester. These cars were expensive. A car in 1901 cost about £390.

German and French manufacturers led the way in developing cars. By 1912 *The Times* was worried about this, and urged the British manufacturer to

set himself seriously to work to produce small cars as good and as cheap as those now imported from abroad.

Strict speed controls were relaxed in Edwardian times and cars steadily improved to become safer, and more reliable and comfortable.

1. What would be the disadvantages in riding in cars like the one in the picture on page 25?
2. What sort of special clothing might drivers and passengers need to wear?

A New Way to Travel

Edwardians saw huge changes in travelling. Not only electric trams, electric underground trains, motor cars, buses and lorries, filled the streets, but a new kind of travelling appeared. In 1909 Bleriot flew an aeroplane from France to England.

1. Where is the engine on this aeroplane?
2. What sort of special clothing did the pilot need?

Early aircraft – like this 1907 machine – were alarmingly fragile. Some were pulled along by their propellors and others were pushed.

7. Votes for Women

Life was hard for women in Edwardian times. Robert Roberts believed that:

Few who were young then will forget the great Friday night scouring ritual in which all the females in the household took part. (Dance halls closed on Friday evenings for lack of girls.) Women wore their lives away washing clothes in heavy iron-hooped tubs, scrubbing wood and stone, polishing furniture and fire irons. Only too well-known was the Saturday morning custom of cleaning and colour-stoning the doorstep.

The Classic Slum

When women went out to work they found that they were paid very low wages. Their wages were much lower than men's.

In 1906 the authors of a study of Birmingham workers reached the conclusion:

Wherever women replaced men the former always received a much lower wage and one that was not proportional to the skill or intelligence required by the work but approximated to a certain fixed level – about 10s.* to 12s. per week, the majority of women getting the lower amount.

(Quoted in *The Edwardian Woman*)

*You will find a note about money on page 3.

Sweated Trades

By 1901 there were laws controlling working conditions in large factories like cotton mills. But in small workshops and in work sent out for people to do in their homes, there were no controls. A committee investigating this kind of work found many women making clothing at wages like those described in this interview by a Mrs Casey

I make shirts at 7d. and 8d. a dozen. I have to pay for my own cotton out of it and I have to pay 2s. 6d. for the machine.
How many shirts can you make in a day?
Two dozen.
What do your materials come to – the cotton and so on you have to find?
About 1s. to 1s. 3d. a week.
How many hours a day do you work?
I begin between 7 and 8 in the morning and I have to work sometimes till 11 at night. I have to attend to the children.

(Quoted in *Human Documents of the Age of the Forsytes*)

1. About how much a week do you think Mrs Casey usually earned?
2. How can you tell she was probably doing this work at home?
3. Why do you think jobs like this were called sweated trades?
4. Can you think of any reasons why employers liked to use women for this sort of work?

Not every job open to women today was

available to them in the 1900s. In 1908 a journalist wrote

She qualifies for the Bar [*the law*], but she is denied the right to practise. She finds there is one standard of payment for men and an inferior one for women.

(Quoted in Read *Edwardian England*)

Votes for Women

By 1901 women could be elected to parish councils, to school boards and boards of guardians of the poor, and in 1907 county and borough politics were opened up to women too. But Parliament was closed to them. They could not vote in elections nor stand as candidates.

But by Edwardian times, Lady Aberdeen saw

Opinion in favour of the suffrage [*right to vote*] is growing very rapidly amongst women, especially since they have been admitted to a local franchise [*the right to vote*].

(Quoted in *Edwardian Scotland*)

Earlier efforts to win women the vote had not attracted much attention. Now there were plenty of people angry about the situation and leaders to guide them. Most famous of all was Mrs Emmeline Pankhurst, founder of the Women's Social and Political Union. Mrs Pankhurst, her daughters Sylvia and Christabel, together with Anne Kenny and

Mrs Pethick Lawrence, made tough speeches and organised women cleverly. In 1908 Mrs Pankhurst explained,

We believe that if we get the vote it will mean better conditions for our unfortunate sisters. The average earnings of the women who earn their living in this country are only 7s. 6d. a week. We have presented larger petitions than were ever presented before. We have succeeded in holding greater public meetings than men have ever had for any reform.

(Quoted in D. Read *Documents*)

1. *How did Mrs Pankhurst's organisation first try and win support?*
2. *What did Mrs Pankhurst suggest women might do with political power?*

Attempts to win enough support peacefully failed. Mr Asquith, Home Secretary 1906–8 and Prime Minister from 1908, was especially hard to convince. When some of Mrs Pankhurst's suffragettes chained themselves to railings near Parliament to win publicity, Asquith said

A man might as well chain himself to the railings of St Thomas's Hospital and say that he will not move until he has a baby.

(Quoted in *Edwardian Scotland*)

Women, as well as men, supported an organisation set up to oppose Mrs Pankhurst.

In songs and in plays, ridicule was poured on suffragettes.

Mrs Pankhurst being arrested outside Buckingham Palace (this photograph is part of a special collection in the Museum of London).

THE CAT AND MOUSE ACT
PASSED BY THE LIBERAL GOVERNMENT

This suffragette poster attacks the Liberal Government's law to deal with hunger-strikers.

Emily Davidson has deliberately thrown herself under the King's horse (on the left) on Derby Day 1913. She died from her injuries.

Put me on an island where the girls are few,
Put me amongst the most ferocious lions in the zoo
You can put me upon a treadmill and I'll never fret,
But for pity's sake don't put me with a suffering-gette.

(Quoted in *The Edwardian Woman*)

Mrs Pankhurst despaired of succeeding through peaceful protest. She decided to try new methods,

I drove in a taxicab accompanied by Mrs Juke and another to No. 10 Downing Street. It was exactly half past five when we alighted from the cab and threw our stones through the windowpanes. As expected we were promptly arrested. At intervals of fifteen minutes relays of women did their work. The first smashing of glass occurred in the Haymarket and Piccadilly. Before the police had reached the station with their prisoners, the splintering of plate glass began again along Regent Street and the Strand. The third relay began breaking the windows in Oxford Circus and Broad Street. Two hundred suffragettes were taken to various police stations.

(Quoted in *They Saw It Happen*)

In 1913 the Speaker of the House of Commons surveyed suffragette activity.

Churches were burnt, public buildings and private residences were destroyed, bombs were exploded, the police and individuals were assaulted, meetings broken up. When offenders were caught and convicted they were sent to prison, but as they generally resorted to a hunger strike and there was a feeling against allowing the law to take its course, they were released and immediately repeated their offences. A Bill was introduced called the Prisoners' Temporary Release Bill, soon nicknamed the 'Cat and Mouse' Bill, to permit the release of offenders on licence; in the event of a subsequent offence the licence should be cancelled. The Bill proved valueless in preventing a continuation of the outrages.

(Quoted in *They Saw It Happen*)

The troubles only stopped with the outbreak of the Great War in 1914.

1. *Explain the reason for the 'Cat and Mouse' Act.*

8. A Better Life

Political Leaders

Most politicians knew there was too much poverty in their country. One of these politicians, Mr Asquith, said,

What is the use of talking about Empire if, here at its centre, there is always to be found a mass of people stunted in education and crowded together beyond the possibility of realising in any true sense either social or domestic life?

Recruiting for the army showed up the poor state of the nation's health. In Manchester, for example, 12000 men volunteered to fight in South Africa, and only 1200 were finally accepted as medically fit, ie one man in ten!

In 1902 the Conservatives began to reform education. In 1906 a Liberal Government was elected which included men keen to tackle the problem of poverty. One of their leaders, David Lloyd George, came from a humble Welsh background. He believed:

If it were found that a Liberal Party had done nothing to cope seriously with the social conditions of the people, to remove the slums and widespread poverty in a land glittering with wealth, then would a real cry arise in this land for a new party.

There was already a small Labour Party to show that Lloyd George might be right. Winston Churchill, another key Liberal figure, came from a very privileged background. But now, a colleague, J. C. Masterman, thought,

He is full of the poor whom he has just discovered. He thinks he is called by Providence to do something for them.

1. *What were the two political parties that ruled Britain in Edwardian times?*
2. *What did the South African war show about the state of Britain's people?*
3. *What was Lloyd George frightened might happen if the Liberals did not attack the problem of poverty?*

Reforms for Children

A local education authority may take such steps as it thinks fit for the provision of meals for children at public elementary schools. Where children are unable by reason of lack of food to take full advantage of education they (the authority) may spend out of the rates.

From the Act of 1906

More and more schools provided meals for needy children. Yet half the local authorities had still not acted by 1913.

Regular medical inspections of schoolchildren began in 1907. In 1912 the Government began to help pay for the school clinics that were gradually appearing. But finding ailments did not solve the problem of treating them.

(above) The Welsh Liberal, David Lloyd George, whose fiery speeches and vigorous reforms so alarmed Conservatives.

Winston Churchill, the former Conservative, whose forceful leadership played a big part in Edwardian politics.

31

In 1908 the Liberals brought in the *Children's Charter*. Begging, smoking and going into public houses were all now forbidden: children on trial were to come before special juvenile courts, and if found guilty could be sent to Borstal (not prison) or put in the care of a probation service.

1. *What did Liberals do to try and improve children's health?*
2. *What reasons can you think of for poor health that could not be solved by doctors?*

Old Age Pensions

In 1908 the Government introduced pensions for elderly people over the age of seventy. Five shillings a week was paid to people who had an income of under £21 a year and who had not been in prison for ten years. Those who had more money of their own received smaller pensions, anyone with over £31 10s. a year did not get a pension at all. There were some grumbles, the Lord Provost of Glasgow said,

It was not those who had been thrifty who were going to be helped but those who had been thriftless.

(Quoted in *Edwardian Scotland*)

But in her village Flora Thompson saw that

When old age pensions began life was transformed for aged cottagers. They were relieved of anxiety. They were suddenly rich.

Independent for life! At first when they went to the Post Office tears of gratitude would run down the cheeks of some and they would say as they picked up their money, 'God bless that *Lord* George and God bless you, miss' and there were flowers from their gardens and apples from their trees for the girls who merely handed them the money.

Lark Rise to Candleford

1. *Who was to claim an old age pension?*
2. *Where was the pension paid?*
3. *Why did some people think the pension wrong?*
4. *What sort of people were likely to think this?*
5. *What happened to very poor elderly people who could not manage before there were pensions? (See Chapter 3 if necessary.)*

The new pension did not provide enough to pay for luxuries. In 1909 the newspaper, *Woman Worker*, described how a Glasgow widow spent her new 5s. old age pension.

It paid for rent, a pint of paraffin for the lamp, a stone [*about 6 kg*] of coal for the fire; a loaf – 2½d.; 2 oz. [*about 56g*] tea – 1s.; 2 lbs [*just under 1 kg*] mutton – 1s.; half a bag of flour – 1d.; pepper, salt and vinegar – 1½d.; beans – ½d.; onions; a herring on Friday – 1d.; cheese for Sunday dinner – 1d.; a pint [*half a litre*] of beer – 1½d. 3¼d. left.

(Quoted in *Edwardian Scotland*)

* You will find a note about money on page 3.

1. *How was the widow's home heated and lit?*
2. *What kinds of meals would she be able to have?*
3. *List any important foods she could not have.*
4. *What would she need the 3¼d. remaining from her week's spending for?*

Unemployment

In 1908 Winston Churchill took action to help. He saw that

the casual labourer who is lucky to get three or four days work in the week, may often be out of a job for three or four weeks at a time, in bad times goes under altogether.

(Quoted in D. Read *Documents*)

Millions of workers had no protection from poverty caused by unemployment. Churchill's first action was to set up, in 1910, Labour Exchanges where jobs could be found, and an insurance scheme.

Under this scheme weekly amounts of 2½d. paid by the employer and employee plus 1⅔d. from the Government provided 7s. a week for up to fifteen weeks.

1. *Where did the money come from for the scheme?*
2. *Would the weekly amounts be enough for a family to live on comfortably?*
3. *What would happen to people out of work for more than fifteen weeks, and to people not in this scheme? (See chapter 3.)*

The first pension day. The elderly were very ready to go to the Post Office for their money.

Health Insurance

Most politicians believed people should save up to pay for medical treatment, and draw on their savings if ill-health put them out of work. But Lloyd George thought

There is a margin of people who cannot be persuaded or cannot afford systematic contributions.

(Quoted in *Human Documents of the Age of Lloyd George*)

There was a long struggle before, finally, in 1911 an act was passed providing ten shillings a week for up to twenty six weeks, with free medical treatment, for workers earning under £160 a year. The money came from weekly payments of 4d. from the employees, 3d. from the employer and 2d. from the Government. The families of insured workers, and other workers, still had to pay for their medical treatment unless they were near to one of the small number of workhouses/infirmaries built to care for the poor who were unwell.

1. *Who did Lloyd George think needed helping in times of illness?*
2. *Who still had to pay for medical care?*

The Battle to win Social Reform

The Liberal reforms did not pass without a struggle. In Parliament Conservatives attacked Liberals for interfering too much in people's lives, and for planning changes that would mean much higher taxes. Lloyd George, as Chancellor of the Exchequer, brought in a budget which proposed:

Income tax to range from 9d. to 1s. 2d. in the pound, (an increase for the better off who had been paying 1s.).
An extra 'supertax' of 6d. in the pound on incomes of over £3000 a year.
Higher duties on beer, spirits, petrol, tobacco.
New taxes on land.

Lloyd George declared

This is a War Budget. It is for raising money to wage warfare against poverty and squalidness. I cannot help hoping that before this generation has passed away we shall have advanced a great step towards that good time when poverty and wretchedness shall be as remote to the people of this country as the wolves that once infested its forests.
(Quoted in *Human Documents of the Age of Lloyd George*)

The Conservative majority in the House of Lords rejected the budget. The furious Liberals called a general election and, when they had won it, the Lords allowed the budget through. After this a bill was passed which stopped the House of Lords from touching bills to do with money. Other bills they could delay for two years, not throw out permanently.

1. *Explain in your own words what Lloyd George meant in his speech about going to war.*

The 'Backwoodsmen are coming to town' (*Punch* cartoon). Lloyd George's plans to tax the wealthy led Conservative members of the House of Lords to turn out in large numbers and vote against them.

9. Changed Days

Trouble in Industry

King Edward VII died in 1910. His son, George V, ruled over a country with many troubles. A journalist wrote of these years:

Underneath our gay social life with its pleasure and pageantry and sport there were signs and sudden outbreaks of ugly conflict. Labour for millions of men and women was underpaid, overworked and insecure. The Welsh miners rioted at Tonypandy. I saw baton charges. There was a general strike in Liverpool. It started with a strike of transport workers and spread to other unions. For many weeks nothing moved in Liverpool. Some troops were sent into the city to maintain order.

(Quoted in *They Saw It Happen*)

London, too, was seriously affected at this time. The dockers' union leader, Ben Tillett, declared,

As a result of the strike of transport workers London was brought within measurable distance of a food famine. We were asking for the dockers a minimum rate of 8d.* and a shilling per hour overtime, a working day from 7 am to 5 pm.

The dockers were successful. Many other strikes of this period were not.

1. *What does the journalist think caused the troubles in industry?*
2. *How much a week, without overtime, were dockers trying to get?*

Wages in the ten years before 1914 did not go up as much as prices. Some workers' leaders agreed with Ben Tillett and Tom Mann that unions should seize a better life for their members.

The statement that the new Trade Unionists look to Government and legislation is bunkum. The keynote is to organize first and take action in the most effective way instead of looking to the Government.

(Quoted in *Life in Edwardian England*)

Small unions began joining together to form bigger unions. For instance, in 1912 the National Union of Railwaymen was formed from three unions. By 1914 the miners, dockers and railwaymen had formed a Triple Alliance to help one another in their disputes. But most disputes were settled, still, without strikes.

1. *What do you think Tillett and Mann wanted workers to do?*

Ben Tillett, the leader of London's dockers, addressing a large meeting during a time of great union activity – the year 1911.

* You will find a note about money on page 3.

35

Trouble in Ireland

In 1914 King George wrote:

For months we have watched with deep misgivings the course of events in Ireland. The trend has been surely and steadily towards an appeal to force and today the cry of Civil War is on the lips of the most responsible and sober-minded of my people.

(Quoted in *Edwardian Scotland*)

Most Irish people wanted Ireland to have her own Parliament, not simply send MPs to Westminster. John Redmond, a Nationalist leader, explained that they wanted, not independence, but home rule.

What we mean by Home Rule is that in the management of all exclusively Irish affairs, Irish public opinion shall be as powerful as the public opinion of Canada or Australia is on the management of their affairs. We rest that claim on historic right, we rest it also on the admitted failure of British government in Ireland.

(Quoted in D. Read *Documents*)

Against the Catholic Nationalists were Protestants led by Sir Edward Carson. Their stronghold lay in the North, in Ulster.

I found Ulster in a state of feverish ferment. The Orangemen [*Protestants*] were passionately rejecting Home Rule for all Ireland both as patriotic Unionists and because they did not wish to be reduced to a minority and feared lest Home Rule meant Rome rule. Many thousands of Volunteers (there were 104000 in all Ulster) marched by while Carson spoke of their determination to stop at nothing rather than be forced out of the Union.

(An Austrian official in *They Saw It Happen*)

By 1914 both sides had organized armies and smuggled in weapons.

1. Explain the meaning of (a) Home Rule
                         (b) Rome Rule.
2. Why were some Irish people against Home Rule?

Anti-Home Rule demonstration led by Sir Edward Carson (with walking stick).

By 1914 the Liberal Government's Home Rule Bill had passed the Commons. The Liberals depended on the votes of Redmond's Nationalists, from 1910, to stay in power. The Conservative leader, Bonar Law, argued that the Government had no business carrying out this change helped by Nationalist votes without another election.

The outbreak of war in Europe, however, halted these events in Ireland. Irishmen from north and south stood together. John Redmond told the House of Commons,

I say to the Government that they may tomorrow withdraw every one of their troops from Ireland. I say that the coast of Ireland will be defended from foreign invasion and for this purpose armed Nationalist Catholics in the South will be only too glad to join arms with armed Protestant Ulstermen in the North.
(Quoted in *Edwardian Scotland*)

Trouble in Europe

Harold Macmillan (a future Prime Minister) was a student at Oxford University in 1914. He remembered:

The First World War burst like a bombshell upon ordinary people. In the summer of 1914 there was far more anxiety about a civil war in Ireland than about a world war in Europe. Had we been told in the summer of 1914 that in a few weeks all our little band of friends would rush to take up arms, that only a few were destined to survive a four years' conflict, we should have thought such prophecies the ravings of a maniac.

The Winds of Change

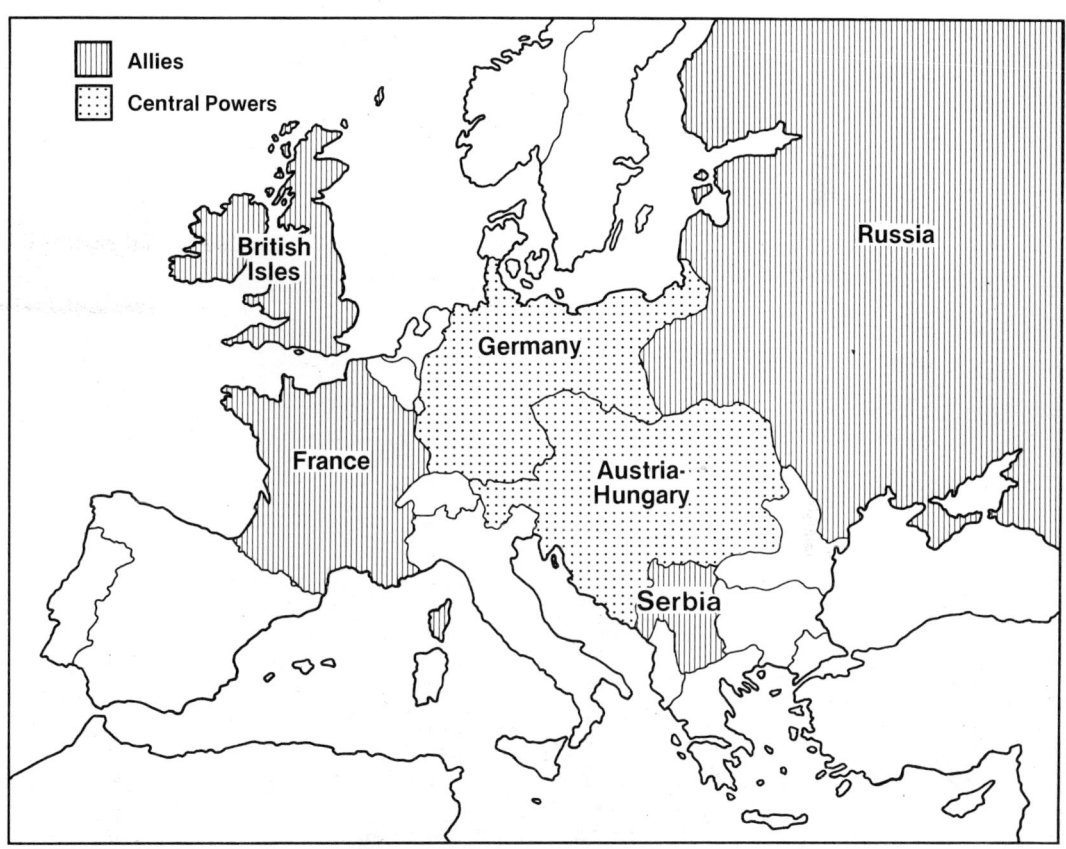

The two sides in 1914.

The King's diary plotted the coming of war.

July 29th Austria has declared war on Serbia. Where will it end? Winston Churchill came to see me, the Navy is all ready for war but please God it will not come.

August 1st Germany declared war on Russia this evening, France is begging us to come to their assistance. At this moment public opinion here is dead against our joining in the war but I think it will be impossible to keep out of it as we cannot allow France to be smashed.

August 3rd Public opinion since Grey made his statement in the House today that we shall not allow Germany to pass through the English Channel and that we should not allow her troops to pass through Belgium, has entirely changed and now every one is for war and helping our friends.

August 4th I held a Council at 10.45 to declare war on Germany, it is a terrible catastrophe but it is not our fault.

(Quoted in Priestley *The Edwardians*)

1. Who was the main enemy on whom Britain declared war?
2. In what year did the First World War begin?
3. Where did war first begin?
4. What changed British opposition to the war?
5. Name one country on the same side as Britain.

Soldiers off to fight in France.

Bibliography and Abbreviation of Sources

Pictorial Books

J. Bishop, *The Illustrated London News Social History of Edwardian Britain*, Angus & Robertson, 1977 (*ILN Social History*)

J. Calder, *The Victorian and Edwardian Home from Old Photographs*, Batsford, 1979

A. B. Demaus, *Victorian and Edwardian Cycling and Motoring*, Batsford, 1977

C. Gordon, *A Richer Dust: Echoes from an Edwardian Album*, Elm Tree Books, 1978

C. W. Hill, *Edwardian Entertainments – a picture postcard view*, M.A.B. Publishing, 1978

C. S. Minto, *Victorian and Edwardian Edinburgh*, Batsford, 1970

J. Spence, *Victorian and Edwardian Railways from Old Photographs*, Batsford, 1977

F. Thompson, *The Victorian and Edwardian Highlands from Old Photographs*, Batsford, 1976

P. Thompson & G. Harkell, *The Edwardians in Photographs*, Batsford, 1979

R. Whitmore, *Victorian and Edwardian Crime and Punishment, from Old Photographs*, Batsford, 1978

G. Winter, *The Golden Years 1903–1913*, David & Charles, 1975 and Penguin, 1977

Documentary Books and Reminiscences

T. Barker, *The Long March of Everyman 1750–1960*, BBC Publications, 1975

R. W. Breach & R. M. Hartwell, *British Economy and Society*, Oxford University Press, 1972

A. Briggs, *They saw it Happen*, Blackwell, 1960

J. Burnet, *Useful Toil*, Penguin, 1977

G. E. Evans, *The Days That We Have Seen*, Faber, 1975

P. Gosden, *How They Were Taught*, Blackwell, 1969

J. R. Hay, *The Development of the British Welfare State 1880–1975*, Arnold, 1978

C. Masterman, *The Condition of England*, Methuen, 1960

K. O. Morgan, *The Age of Lloyd George*, Allen & Unwin, 1971

D. Read, *Documents from Edwardian England*, Harrap, 1973 (D. Read *Documents*)

R. Roberts, *The Classic Slum* and *A Ragged Schooling*, Manchester University Press, 1971 and 1976

E. Royston Pike, *Human Documents of the Age of the Forsytes* and *Human Documents of the Lloyd George Era*, Allen & Unwin, 1970 and 1972

P. Thompson, *The Edwardians*, Paladin, 1977

General Histories

R. Cecil, *Life in Edwardian England*, Batsford, 1969

R. C. K. Ensor, *England 1870–1914*, Oxford University Press, 1936

S. Nowell-Smith, *Edwardian England*, Oxford University Press, 1964

J. B. Priestley, *The Edwardians*, Heinemann, 1970

D. Read, *Edwardian England 1901–1915*, Harrap, 1972

L. C. B. Seaman, *Post-Victorian Britain 1902–51*, Methuen, 1967

B. Tuchman, *The Proud Tower*, Hamish Hamilton, 1966

Special Studies

A. Adburgham, *Shopping in Style*, Thames & Hudson, 1979

J. Camplin, *The Rise of the Plutocrats: Wealth and Power in Edwardian England*, Constable, 1978

D. Crow, *The Edwardian Woman*, Allen & Unwin, 1978

C. W. Hill, *Edwardian Scotland*, Scottish Academic Press, 1976

S. Hynes, *The Edwardian Turn of Mind*, Princeton University Press, 1968

N. Longmate, *The Workhouse*, Temple Smith, 1974

S. Maclure, *100 Years of London Education 1870–1970*, Allen Lane, 1970

S. Meacham, *A Life Apart*, Thames & Hudson, 1977

K. Middlemas, *The Life and Times of Edward VII*, Weidenfeld and Nicholson, 1972

D. Richards & J. Woodward, *Health Care and Popular Medicine in Nineteenth Century England*, Croom Helm, 1977

G. St Aubyn, *Edward VII, Prince and King*, Collins, 1979

A. Sproule, *The Social Calendar*, Blandford Press, 1978

J. K. Walton, *The Blackpool Landlady*, Manchester University Press, 1978

J. Walvin, *Beside the Seaside*, Allen Lane, 1978